Grasslands

by Susan H. Gray

Content Adviser: Terrence E. Young Jr., M.Ed., M.L.S.,
Jefferson Parish (La.) Public Schools

Reading Adviser: Dr. Linda D. Labbo,
Department of Reading Education, College of Education,
The University of Georgia

COMPASS POINT BOOKS

Minneapolis, Minnesota

Compass Point Books
3722 West 50th Street, #115
Minneapolis, MN 55410

Visit Compass Point Books on the Internet at *www.compasspointbooks.com* or e-mail your request
to *custserv@compasspointbooks.com*

Photographs ©:Root Resources/Kohout Productions, cover; Robert McCaw, 4, 5; John Gerlach/Tom Stack and Associates,
6; Cartesia, 7; John Shaw/Tom Stack and Associates, 8; James P. Rowan, 9; Index Stock Imagery, 10; James P. Rowan, 11 top;
Root Resources/Kohout Productions, 11 bottom; James P. Rowan, 12 left; Unicorn Stock Photos/Susan McGee, 12 right;
Visuals Unlimited/Ron Spomer, 13; Visuals Unlimited/John D. Cunningham, 14; James L. Shaffer, 15; Visuals Unlimited/Bob
Clay, 16 top; Visuals Unlimited/Mark E. Gibson, 16 bottom; Visuals Unlimited/Nancy M. Wells, 17; Visuals Unlimited/R.
Calentine, 18; Visuals Unlimited/Dan Richter, 21; W. Perry Conway/Tom Stack and Associates, 22; Ken W. Davis/Tom Stack
and Associates, 23; Diana L. Stratton/Tom Stack and Associates, 24; Richard Hamilton Smith, 25; James P. Rowan, 27;
Thomas Kitchin/Tom Stack and Associates, 28 top; Joe McDonald/Tom Stack and Associates, 28 bottom; Dave Watts/Tom
Stack and Associates, 29; John Shaw/Tom Stack and Associates, 30 top; Root Resources/Ben Goldstein, 30 bottom; Stan
Osolinksi/FPG International, 31; Root Resources/Pat Wadecki, 32; Root Resources/Alan G. Nelson, 33; James P. Rowan, 35;
Alan Kearney/FPG International, 36; Inga Spence/Tom Stack and Associates, 37; Tom Stack/Tom Stack and Associates, 39;
AP/Wide World Photos/Arthur Rothstein, 40; Werner Forman/Corbis, 41; Index Stock Imagery, 42.

Editors: E. Russell Primm and Emily J. Dolbear
Photo Researcher: Svetlana Zhurkina
Photo Selector: Dawn Friedman
Design: Bradfordesign, Inc.

Library of Congress Cataloging-in-Publication Data
Gray, Susan Heinrichs.
   Grasslands / by Susan H. Gray.
      p. cm. — (First reports)
   Includes bibliographical references and index.
   Summary: Briefly describes different types of grasslands, their plant and animal life, and envi-
ronmental threats.
      ISBN 0-7565-0020-6 (hardcover : lib. bdg.)
      1. Grassland ecology—Juvenile literature. 2. Grasslands—Juvenile literature. [1. Grassland
ecology. 2. Ecology. 3. Grasslands.] I. Title. II. Series.
   QH541.5.P7 G76 2000
   577.4—dc21   00-008530

Table of Contents

What Goes on in a Grassland?

▲ *Grasslands are called prairies in North America.*

At first glance, it looks as if nothing much goes on in a grassland. The grasses wave gently in the breeze. Animals quietly feed on the grasses. Birds cling to tall stalks as they sing their morning songs. No one would imagine that millions of **rodents** are busy creating towns here. No one would picture a wildfire roaring across this

▲ *A vesper sparrow singing in a Canadian grassland*

peaceful land. No one would guess that owls are scuttling about underground. But these are grassland scenes too.

The Earth's Grasslands

▲ *A herd of wildebeest in an African savanna*

Grasslands cover about one-fourth of Earth's land area. They are either large, flat lands or areas with rolling hills. There are at least two kinds of grasslands. Temperate grasslands are called simply grasslands. Tropical grasslands are called **savannas**.

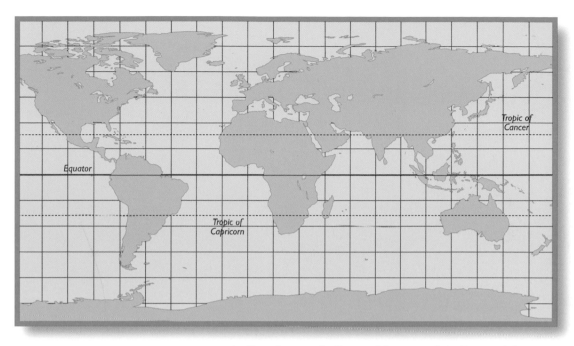

▲ Map showing the Tropic of Cancer and the Tropic of Capricorn

Most of the world's temperate grasslands lie north of an imaginary line around the Earth called the Tropic of Cancer. The Tropic of Cancer is the northern boundary of the world's tropics. A few grasslands lie south of another imaginary line around the Earth called the Tropic of Capricorn. The Tropic of Capricorn is the southern boundary of the world's tropics. Savannas lie between these two lines.

Grasslands get 10 to 30 inches (25 to 76 centimeters) of rain a year. Savannas get 4 to 65 inches (10 to
165 centimeters) of rain a year. Unlike grasslands,
savannas have wet and dry seasons.

Grasslands have many different types of grasses, a
few woody shrubs, and many different wildflowers.
Prairie coneflowers, Texas bluebonnets, and locoweed

▲ *Bluebonnets and paintbrush bloom in a Texas prairie.*

▲ Trees on the savanna in Masai Mara National Park, Kenya

cover the land with gold, blue, and purple. Scattered trees dot savannas. Very few trees are found in grass-lands.

Grasslands cover a large part of Europe and Asia, where they are called **steppes**. In Argentina, they are called **pampas**. In North America, grasslands stretch

▲ Grasslands in Nepal, near China

▼ *A shortgrass prairie in Colorado*　　　　　　　　▲ *A tallgrass prairie in Illinois*

from Canada into Mexico. In the East, grasslands are called tallgrass prairies. In the West, they are called shortgrass prairies, or plains.

▲ Blue grama grass

▲ Indian grass

In the East, grasses such as Indian grass and big bluestem grow 10 feet (3 meters) high. Western grasses are usually no more than 1 foot (30 centimeters) high. Buffalo and blue grama grasses grow here. A middle area, called the mixed-grass prairie, has tall, short, and medium-sized plants.

▲ *A mixed-grass prairie in South Dakota*

What Exactly Are Grasses?

▲ *Grass roots help hold soil together.*

Grasses are plants with thin leaves and tiny flowers. Their roots keep soil from washing away in the rain. They can survive cutting, burning, and trampling.

Their leaves make grasses special. The leaves of other plants grow from their tips. If the tips are broken off, the leaf stops growing. The leaves of grasses grow from their bases, however. So when animals chew off the tips, the grasses keep growing.

Earth has about 9,000 different kinds of grasses. That includes the grasses that grow in people's lawns. It also includes sugarcane, bamboo, rice, wheat, and corn.

▲ *When most people think of grass, they think of lawns.*

Sugarcane

A bamboo grove

16

▲ *A sod house*

Grasses either form mats or grow in bunches. Mat grasses spread out to cover large areas. They have thick root systems that cling tightly to the soil. Soil bound into a thick mat by grass and plant roots is called **sod**.

American pioneers in the 1800s discovered an unusual use for sod. They dug it up in big blocks.

▲ *The roots and underground stems of a nut sedge*

Then they stacked the blocks into walls and added a roof. These sod houses provided homes for many early settlers.

Bunch grasses grow in clumps between other types of plants. Many grasses spread through their underground stems. These underground stems grow up and down. They send roots down into the ground and new shoots up.

Where Does Soil Come From?

When grasses die and fall to the ground, they decay, or **decompose**, and become soil. Small living things called bacteria, single-celled animals called protozoa, and insects such as beetles break down the dead grass. The mixture of dead grass and animals is called **humus**. It may take several years for the grasses to break down completely.

Humus is full of food sources called **nutrients**. Each year a new batch of grass grows up and then dies. Over time, the humus piles up. It forms a thick, black layer that holds water and feeds new plants.

▲ *Rich humus soil in a spring field*

Fires in the Grasslands

▲ *A prairie fire in eastern Colorado*

Sometimes grasslands get no rain for a long time. The blades of grass become crisp and dry. Then dark clouds form and lightning strikes. It sparks a fire that sweeps over the land. Soon rain puts the fire out or the fire burns itself out.

▲ *The blackened ground of a California grass fire*

Fire blackens the whole area. It seems like a terrible thing. But this fire helps to renew the land.

When too much humus builds up, the ground below it does not get enough air and sunlight. But when a fire starts, it burns up most of the humus layer. This releases more nutrients into the ground. It also

▲ *New grasses growing after a fire in Yellowstone National Park*

allows air and sunlight to reach the soil. After the fire, humus begins building up again.

It looks as if fires destroy grasslands. But the underground stems of the grasses are alive and growing. Soon they send up new shoots and the land is green again.

Woody bushes and trees are completely burned up. In time, new trees and bushes will grow. If they were not destroyed, they would take over the grass-lands.

For years, people tried to put out grassland fires as soon as they started. They were afraid that fires would wipe out all the grasses. They did not realize how helpful fires were.

▲ *Setting a controlled prairie fire in Minnesota*

Today, people in charge of grasslands start fires on purpose! They set long rows of grass on fire and let the fire burn. New grass shoots appear within days. However, sometimes, the fire gets out of control and reaches areas where people live.

Grassland Animals

▲ *A young grasshopper living in an Illinois prairie*

Grasslands support all kinds of animals. Worms wriggle through the soil, breaking it up so that air seeps through. Beetles help decompose soil in the humus layer. There are also grasshoppers, flies, ants, spiders, and bees. The numbers of insects are highest in the summer and fall.

The only birds that live in grasslands are birds that nest on the ground. Sparrows, meadowlarks, bobolinks, and hawks build nests here.

▲ *Western grey kangaroos feeding in southern Australia's grassland*

On the grassland, large animals eat the grass. They are usually fast runners or jumpers. Kangaroos feed on Australia's grasslands. Their powerful hind legs let them leap away when fires rage across the land.

A bison herd grazing in South Dakota   ▲ A pronghorn antelope

Buffalo, or bison, and pronghorns live on North American grasslands. In the past, hunters killed almost all these animals. Now, herds of thousands drift across the shortgrass prairies. Pronghorns look like antelopes but they are not even closely related. They are the fastest animals in North America. When a pronghorn is alarmed, it can move at 60 miles (96 kilometers) an hour.

Gazelles and cheetahs live on the plains of Africa. The cheetah is the fastest of all land animals. It can

▲ *A cheetah leaping*

go from a standing position to 70 miles (113 kilometers) per hour in three seconds.

Many prairie dogs live in the North American shortgrass prairies. These rodents dig tunnels called **burrows** that go straight down. Then the tunnels branch off into little nesting areas. Sometimes, thou-

△ *Prairie dogs*

sands of these rodents live together in large groups called prairie dog towns.

Sometimes other small animals take over prairie dog towns. Rattlesnakes and weasels slip through the burrows looking for a meal. Burrowing owls also use tunnels left by prairie dogs. They scratch out the

▲ *Burrowing owls*

holes to make them bigger. When they find the nesting area, the female owl lays her eggs. Baby burrowing owls hatch underground. Their parents feed them for about six weeks before the babies leave the nest.

Some Problems with Farms and Ranches

▲ Corn fields on a Wisconsin farm

Farmers like grasslands because the soil is full of nutrients and crops grow so easily there. Corn and wheat grow as well as the natural grasses. And ranchers like grasslands because they provide excellent food for sheep and cattle.

When farmers mow their crops, there are problems. Birds that nest on the ground are no longer protected. The layer of humus gets pressed down and no air can get through. When farmers plant the same

▲ *Harvesting wheat with heavy machines like combines can harm grasslands.*

▲ *A herd of Jersey cows graze in a California pasture.*

crops over and over, all the soil's nutrients get used up.

As long as the ranchers raise only a few sheep and cattle, grasslands can survive. In fact, plants respond by growing faster. But when ranchers bring in large herds of animals, the grassland suffers. The animals stamp down the grass and humus. They eat up the grass faster than it can grow. And to protect their animals, herd owners put out grass fires that might be good for the grasslands.

What Happens When People Overuse Grasslands?

▲ *A dust storm in former farm land in New Mexico*

When people overuse grasslands, the area often turns into a desert. In the early 1900s, many Americans settled in the grasslands of Kansas, Oklahoma, Texas, New Mexico, and Colorado. They planted wheat and

△ *An Arkansas farmer and his children in the Dust Bowl, 1936*

raised cattle. But the soil was slowly losing nutrients and blowing away. Then, in the 1930s, the weather became very dry. More soil blew away and the land became useless. The winds were so dusty that people called it the Dust Bowl. Thousands of families had to leave.

After that, people treated the land differently. Grasses were planted and farmers began planting different crops to improve the soil. The Dust Bowl did not quite become a desert. Sadly, some grasslands in Africa have become deserts though.

The Sahara is a huge desert in Africa. A region just south of the Sahara, known as the Sahel, is a savanna. It receives less than 8 inches (20 centimeters) of rain a

▲ *The Sahel is an African desert that used to be a grassland.*

year. When people began driving more and more herds over the land, the grass started to disappear. Between the 1960s and 1980s, there was a severe **drought**—a time without rain. Grasses, crops, and animals died. Many people starved. The savanna had become a desert.

▲ *Thriving grasslands in Ethiopia*

Now the United Nations has a group of experts trying to stop this misuse of land. They work with communities to keep other areas from becoming deserts. They know it is important to save grasslands all over the world.

Glossary

burrows—tunnels under the ground

decompose—to break down dead plants and animals

drought—dry period

humus—dead grass and decomposing animals

nutrients—the materials a living thing needs to live and grow

pampas—grasslands in Argentina

rodents—animals with large teeth for gnawing or nibbling, such as prairie dogs, rats, or beavers

savannas—tropical grasslands

sod—the top layer of soil and the attached grass

steppes—grasslands in Europe and Asia

Did You Know?

- Grasses such as wheat, oats, barley, and corn are used to make bread, pastes, and plastics.

- Dogs sometimes eat grass to cure a stomachache. The grass makes the dogs vomit, which makes them feel better.

- Even when it is dry, a lawn should not be watered more than once a week.

At a Glance

Location: Parts of Africa, South America, Australia (savannas); central North America and central Asia (temperate grasslands)

Amount of rain or snow each year: 36 to 60 inches (91 to 152 centimeters) (savannas); 4 to 24 inches (10 to 61 centimeters) (temperate grasslands)

Description: Open grassy plains with a long dry season and a short rainy season (savannas); rich soil with tall, dense grasses and scattered trees (temperate grasslands)

Common animals: Lions, elephants, giraffes, cheetahs, gazelles (savannas); bison, prairie dogs, pronghorns, wolves, coyotes, black-footed ferrets (temperate grasslands)

Common plants: Grasses and scattered trees (savannas); buffalo and blue grama grasses (temperate grasslands)

Want to Know More?

At the Library

Knapp, Brian J. *What Do We Know about Grasslands?* New York: Peter Bedrick Books, 1992.

Pipes, Rose. *Grasslands.* Austin, Tex.: Raintree Steck-Vaughn, 1998.

Ricciuti, Edward R. *Grassland.* New York: Benchmark Books, 1996.

Savage, Stephen. *Animals of the Grasslands.* Austin, Tex: Raintree Steck-Vaughn, 1997.

On the Web

Grassland Animals

http://mbgnet.mobot.org/sets/grasslnd/animals/index.htm

For an introduction to the animals that live in grassland regions from the Evergreen Project

The Grassland Biome

http://lsb.syr.edu/projects/cyberzoo/biomes/grass.html

For information about geological events, weather, and animals in grasslands

Through the Mail

National Grasslands Visitor Center

708 Main Street, P.O. Box 425

Wall, SD 57790

For information about the promotion of grasslands

On the Road

Grasslands National Park

P.O. Box 150

Val Marie, Saskatchewan

Canada S0N 2T0

http://parkscanada.pch.gc.ca/parks/saskatchewan/grasslands/

For information about visiting a mixed-grass prairie

Index

About the Author

Susan H. Gray holds bachelor's and master's degrees in zoology from the University of Arkansas in Fayetteville. She has taught classes in general biology, human anatomy, and physiology. She has also worked as a freshwater biologist and scientific illustrator. In her twenty years as a writer, Susan H. Gray has covered many topics and written a variety of science books for children.